USING CARBON SINKS
TO FIGHT CLIMATE CHANGE
by Cynthia Kennedy Henzel

FOCUS
READERS.
NAVIGATOR

WWW.FOCUSREADERS.COM

Focus Readers is distributed by North Star Editions:
sales@northstareditions.com | 888-417-0195

Produced for Focus Readers by Red Line Editorial.

Content Consultant: Ning Zeng, PhD, Professor of Atmospheric and Oceanic Science, University of Maryland

Photographs ©: Shutterstock Images, cover, 1, 8–9, 11, 17, 19, 22–23, 27; KSC/NASA, 4–5; Jeff Schmaltz/MODIS Land Rapid Response Team/GSFC/NASA, 7; Red Line Editorial, 13; Scott Johnson/National Park Service, 14–15; UNCW Mohawk ROV/NOAA Ship Nancy Foster/John Bilotta/U. of Minnesota Ext and Sea Grant Programs/NOAA, 21; Mikhail Kanevskiy/INE University of Alaska Fairbanks/USGS, 25; Climeworks/Cover Images/AP Images, 29

Library of Congress Cataloging-in-Publication Data
Library of Congress Cataloging-in-Publication Data is available on the Library of Congress website.

ISBN
978-1-63739-275-1 (hardcover)
978-1-63739-327-7 (paperback)
978-1-63739-426-7 (ebook pdf)
978-1-63739-379-6 (hosted ebook)

Printed in the United States of America
Mankato, MN
082022

ABOUT THE AUTHOR

Cynthia Kennedy Henzel has a BS in social studies education and an MS in geography. She has worked as a teacher-educator in many countries. Currently, she writes fiction and nonfiction books and develops education materials for social studies, history, science, and ELL students. She has written more than 100 books and more than 150 stories for young people.

TABLE OF CONTENTS

CHAPTER 1

WATCHING EARTH

MODIS is watching Earth. Every one to two days, this instrument flies around the planet. It watches everything, including rainforests and cities. It flies on a satellite called Terra. MODIS measures plant growth. It finds fires and volcanoes. It measures Earth's temperature. It measures water in the atmosphere.

Terra launched into space in 1999.

Scientists use this data to understand carbon sinks and carbon sources. A carbon sink is anything that stores more carbon than it gives off. For example, plants are carbon sinks. The ocean is the largest carbon sink.

In contrast, carbon sources add carbon dioxide (CO_2) to the atmosphere. Some of this gas is released when living things die. People also release CO_2 by burning oil or coal. Extra CO_2 in the atmosphere heats the planet. It causes **climate change**.

As Earth warms, ice melts. Ocean levels rise. Droughts and floods increase. Storms get more harmful. CO_2 in the atmosphere is the main cause of

In 2011, MODIS studied phytoplankton in an Arctic sea. These organisms help the ocean store carbon.

climate change. MODIS helps scientists understand how much CO_2 is in different carbon sinks. Then they make **models** of how Earth changes. Those models help better track the climate crisis.

CHAPTER 2

CARBON AND CLIMATE

Carbon is an **element**. The amount of carbon on Earth stays the same. But it moves and changes forms. Plants take CO_2 out of the air during **photosynthesis**. Then plants store the carbon. Animals that eat plants store carbon, too.

Carbon from dead plants and animals forms underground sinks. Some carbon

During photosynthesis, plants use CO_2, light energy, and water. Plants turn the CO_2 into a sugar known as glucose.

becomes fossil fuels, such as oil and coal. Other carbon is stored in limestone. Limestone is a type of rock formed when shells and bones press together. Over time, underground carbon returns to the atmosphere. This can happen through volcanoes. Or it can happen when rocks move to the surface.

This whole process is known as the carbon cycle. It shows how carbon moves between the atmosphere, the land, and the oceans.

Having a certain amount of CO_2 in the atmosphere is important for life on Earth. That's because CO_2 is a **greenhouse gas**. Greenhouse gases trap heat from the sun.

Without greenhouse gases, Earth would freeze. But with too much, Earth could get far too hot.

THE CARBON CYCLE

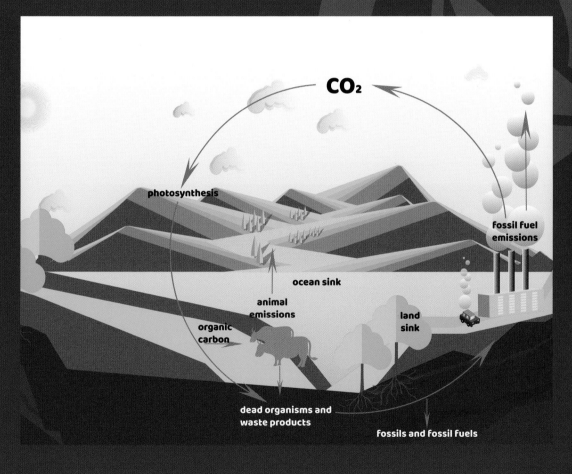

Over many years, people added CO_2 to the atmosphere by burning huge amounts of fossil fuels. The amount of CO_2 in the atmosphere shot up. Earth got warmer.

People are also destroying large carbon sinks. They are cutting trees for wood. They are burning forests to make space for farming. These actions release stored

FROM SINK TO SOURCE

The Amazon is the largest rainforest on Earth. It has also been one of the largest carbon sinks. But the Amazon is shrinking. As more forest is lost, the soil releases more CO_2. For this reason, scientists believe the Amazon rainforest might not be a carbon sink anymore. Instead, it might be a source.

carbon into the atmosphere. As a result, climate change is becoming worse at a faster rate.

CARBON SOURCES AND SINKS

The top of this graph shows how much CO_2 people have produced. The bottom shows how much was absorbed.

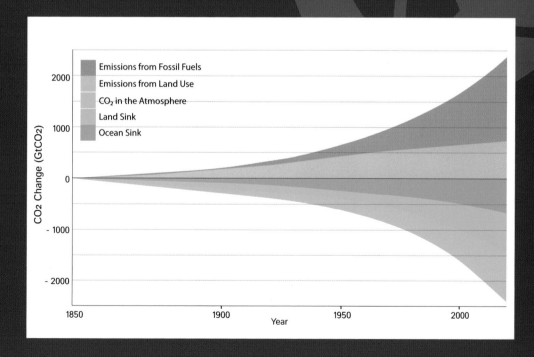

CHAPTER 3

BETTER CARBON SINKS

Scientists are working to improve the health of existing carbon sinks. Some scientists use small fires to control brush. These fires help prevent large wildfires. That keeps the forest alive and healthy.

Scientists are also finding out which **biomes** are the best carbon sinks. This helps them know which areas to protect.

A member of the US Forest Service helps manage a controlled burn in Mississippi's Tombigbee National Forest.

For example, mangroves are areas where trees and bushes grow in warm, salty water. Mangroves are important sinks. Seagrass along ocean shores also helps store carbon. It is stored in ocean silt. Peatlands are strong sinks, too. They hold partly broken-down vegetation. Peatlands store twice as much carbon as forests.

Many carbon sinks are already damaged. But some can be restored. Areas can be replanted with native vegetation. Laws can protect other sinks. That way, these areas have a chance to recover on their own. People can also make new carbon sinks. They can plant trees in natural and urban areas.

Given the same space, mangroves can store four times more carbon than rainforests.

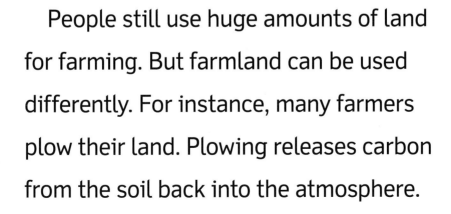

People still use huge amounts of land for farming. But farmland can be used differently. For instance, many farmers plow their land. Plowing releases carbon from the soil back into the atmosphere.

In response, scientists have invented new types of crops. These crops do not need plowing. As a result, less carbon is lost from the soil.

Grassland can also be a carbon sink. However, ranchers often pack too many cattle into one area. Then the cattle trample the soil and kill the grass. When

PLANTING TREES

Trees take in carbon. However, planting more trees might not be enough to stop climate change. Planting 500 billion trees would capture 20 years of human-made CO_2. But that many trees would cover more than the whole United States. Even so, planting trees can still play an important role.

Many traditional herding practices can help land store carbon.

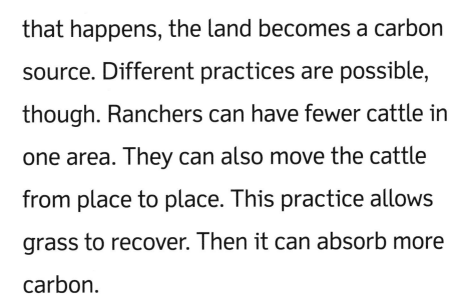

that happens, the land becomes a carbon source. Different practices are possible, though. Ranchers can have fewer cattle in one area. They can also move the cattle from place to place. This practice allows grass to recover. Then it can absorb more carbon.

MARINE SNOW

Marine snow is not really snow. It begins as bits of living things at the ocean's surface. When these living things die, they sink toward the ocean floor. The fluffy white bits may clump together as they sink. They get larger until they look like snowflakes. Many creatures in the deep sea eat the marine snow. Much of the snow lands on the bottom of the ocean. It makes a muddy slime.

Scientists discovered that marine snow is an important carbon sink. The snow adds hundreds of millions of tons of carbon to the slime each year. The carbon may stay on the ocean floor for hundreds of years. It may even become part of rocks below the ocean floor.

Marine snow falls to the seafloor where many fish gather.

CHAPTER 4

THE PATH AHEAD

By the 2020s, CO_2 levels in the atmosphere were dangerously high. And people were still producing billions of tons of CO_2 every year. Most of that came from burning fossil fuels. Thankfully, carbon sinks took in nearly half of what people released. Even so, too much CO_2 was entering the air.

In the early 2020s, coal supplied approximately one-quarter of the world's energy.

Many scientists worried the climate was heading toward serious tipping points. A tipping point happens when small changes create a sudden, massive shift.

Some tipping points involve carbon sinks. For example, the Arctic tundra is an important carbon sink. The tundra soil is frozen during much of the year. It is known as permafrost. Frozen soil slows plants from breaking down. The carbon then stays stored in the ground. But as the planet warms, more tundra thaws. The tundra could suddenly become a carbon source. That shift could quickly make climate change much worse.

A wall of permafrost thaws along the Itkillik River in Alaska.

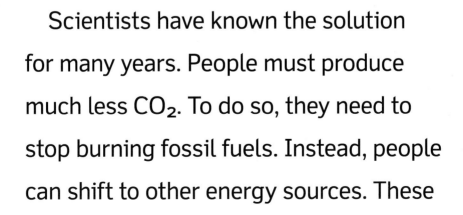

Scientists have known the solution for many years. People must produce much less CO_2. To do so, they need to stop burning fossil fuels. Instead, people can shift to other energy sources. These sources include wind power, solar power, and nuclear power.

Most of the technology to reduce CO_2 already exists. However, it is not easy for companies and governments to make

INDIGENOUS PEOPLES

Indigenous peoples manage 18 percent of all the world's land. This land includes 1.2 billion acres (486 million ha) of forest. Indigenous scientists often best understand local biomes. After all, Indigenous peoples have worked their lands for thousands of years. However, countries and companies do not always respect their land rights. Many scientists argue that Indigenous peoples should have more power over their lands. They can protect many of the world's best carbon sinks.

An Indigenous Siona woman harvests a yucca plant in the Ecuadorian Amazon.

huge changes. So, scientists are working to give people more time to change. They are exploring new ways to take carbon out of the atmosphere.

Some work on improving natural carbon sinks. One idea is to add iron to the ocean. This element makes **plankton** grow faster. When the plankton die, they sink to the bottom of the ocean. They can store carbon for thousands of years.

Other scientists have suggested using cold water from deep in the ocean. People could bring that water to the surface. This would cool the ocean surface. Cooler water can store more CO_2.

Still other scientists are developing human-made carbon sinks. One of these sinks uses a different kind of concrete. The concrete stores carbon. Another idea is to capture CO_2 from factories. Then the carbon can be buried. That way, the carbon would not enter the atmosphere.

In 2021, the largest carbon capture plant took in the amount of CO_2 that 250 Americans produce every year.

As of the early 2020s, scientists did not know how much these solutions could help. They might even cause bigger problems. Even so, scientists were working to give people as much time as possible.

FOCUS ON
USING CARBON SINKS

Write your answers on a separate piece of paper.

1. Write a sentence describing the main ideas of Chapter 2.

2. Would you like to help restore a damaged carbon sink? Why or why not?

3. What is the largest carbon sink on Earth?

    A. the Amazon rainforest

    B. the ocean

    C. the Arctic tundra

4. Planting trees in an urban area is an example of what action?

    A. protecting an existing carbon sink

    B. restoring a damaged carbon sink

    C. creating a new carbon sink

Answer key on page 32.

GLOSSARY

biomes
Large natural environments with particular communities of plants and animals.

climate change
A human-caused global crisis involving long-term changes in Earth's temperature and weather patterns.

element
A pure substance, made of only one kind of atom.

greenhouse gas
A gas that traps heat in Earth's atmosphere, causing climate change.

Indigenous
Native to a region, or belonging to ancestors who lived in a region before colonists arrived.

models
Math equations and data used to describe how systems work.

photosynthesis
The process in which plants turn sunlight, carbon dioxide, and water into oxygen and energy.

plankton
Tiny creatures that often drift in big swarms in the ocean.

TO LEARN MORE

BOOKS

McCarthy, Cecilia Pinto. *Capturing Carbon with Fake Trees*. Minneapolis: Abdo Publishing, 2020.

Minoglio, Andrea. *Our World Out of Balance: Understanding Climate Change and What We Can Do*. San Francisco: Blue Dot Kids Press, 2021.

Tate, Nikki. *If a Tree Falls: The Global Impact of Deforestation*. Custer, WA: Orca Book Publishers, 2020.

NOTE TO EDUCATORS

Visit **www.focusreaders.com** to find lesson plans, activities, links, and other resources related to this title.

INDEX

USING CARBON SINKS
TO FIGHT CLIMATE CHANGE
by Cynthia Kennedy Henzel

FOCUS
READERS®

NAVIGATOR